Oscar Wilde's
DORIAN GRAY

Oscar Wilde's
DORIAN GRAY

adapted for the stage by

Mike Parker

WordCrafts
Theatrical Press

CAUTION: Professionals and amateurs are hereby warned that performance of **Oscar Wilde's Dorian Gray** is subject to payment of a royalty. It is fully protected under the copyright laws of the United States of America, and of all countries covered by the International Copyright Union. All rights, including professional, amateur, motion picture, public reading, broadcast, and any other reproduction by means known or yet to be discovered are strictly reserved.

All rights are controlled exclusively by WordCrafts Theatrical Press, 912 East Lincoln Street, Tullahoma, Tennessee 37388. No performance of this play may be given without obtaining in advance the written permission of WordCrafts Theatrical Press, and paying the requisite fee.

SPECIAL NOTE: Anyone receiving permission to produce **Oscar Wilde's Dorian Gray** is required to give credit to the Author as the sole and exclusive Author of the Play on the title page of all programs distributed in connection with performances of the Play and in all instances in which the title of the Play appears for purposes of advertising, publicizing or otherwise exploiting the Play. The name of the Author must appear on a separate line, in which no other name appears, immediately beneath the title and in size of type equal to 50% of the size of the largest, most prominent letter used for the title of the Play. No person, firm or entity may receive credit larger or more prominent than that accorded the Author.

Oscar Wilde's Dorian Gray
Copyright © 2003
Mike Parker

Cover art by Vassiliki Koutsothanasi
Used by permission

All rights reserved. No part of this book may be reproduced, stored in a retrieval system, or transmitted in any form or by any means – electronic, mechanical, photocopy, recording, or otherwise – without the prior written permission of the publisher. The only exception is brief quotations for review purposes.

Published by WordCrafts Theatrical Press
912 E. Lincoln St.
Tullahoma, TN 37388
www.wordcrafts.net

For all my girls:
> *"Charm is deceitful, and beauty is vain..."*

Playwright's Notes:

In the preface to his only novel, 19th Century English playwright, Oscar Wilde commented, "All art is at once surface and symbol. Those who go beneath the surface do so at their own peril. Those who read the symbol do so at their peril."

That novel, **The Picture of Dorian Gray**, is undoubtedly a work of art, filled with both surface and symbol. It is also a work of exquisite beauty. Few writers of any era can match Wilde for his marvelous manipulation of the English language. And yet, there is something more; something almost autobiographical about this curious retelling of the Faust myth. For those who would hazard to look beneath the surface to read the symbol - be careful. You might find in it the autobiography of your own soul.

An adherent to the pseudo-religion of aestheticism, a philosophy that worships beauty above all things, Wilde used **The Picture of Dorian Gray** to explore the breadth and depth of that peculiar faith. In the end, Oscar Wilde, along with his creation, Dorian Gray, discovered that beauty is a gift, but only for a season. "The pulse of joy that beats in us at twenty becomes sluggish," Lord Henry asserts. "Our limbs fail, our senses rot. We degenerate into hideous puppets." King Solomon, perhaps, said it better, "Vanity of vanities. All is vanity."

In adapting **Dorian Gray** for the stage, I have taken some literary license. I beg the forgiveness of Mr. Wilde and of all English Lit teachers everywhere.

The first, and most striking change I made was in recasting the genders of several pivotal characters, most notably that of Dorian Gray. In contemporary society it is not much of a challenge to show a man traveling down the road to perdition. Indeed, it seems almost expected. There is something more intriguing when a beautiful young woman chooses that path.

There is an old saying that declares, *As a man sows, so shall he also reap.*

Ultimately, that is what my play, **Oscar Wilde's Dorian Gray**, is all about - sowing and reaping. And a lifeline in the darkness. And our choice whether to reach for it or not. As Oscar Wilde himself so eloquent wrote, "It is the confession, not the priest, that gives us absolution."

Readers will note that I have intentionally kept stage directions to a minimum. Hopefully this will give the director freedom to 'direct.'

Mike Parker, playwright

Oscar Wilde's
DORIAN GRAY

Characters
(In Order of Appearance)

Basil Hallward: A young man. An artist. A member of the Pre-Raphaelite Brotherhood.

Lady Harriett Wotten: A young woman. Basil's older sister.

Parker: Basil Hallward's servant.

Dorian Gray: A young woman, not yet 18.

Lord George Fermor: Older gentleman. Harriett's uncle.

Lady Marguerite de Navarre: A young woman. A socialite.

John Vane: A young man. An actor.

Mrs. Vane: An older woman. John's mother.

Sibyl Vane: A child. John's sister.

Alice: A young woman. Dorian's housekeeper.

Lady Penelope Narborough: An older woman.

Berwick: Alan Campbell. Duke of Berwick. A young man.

Lady Jayne Ruxton: An older woman.

Sibyl Vane: (older) John's sister, 40 years later.

ACT I
Scene 1

SETTING: London - In the Year of our Lord, 1870. BASIL HALLWARD'S studio, furnished comfortably in the style of the day with a divan, a chair, an occasional table, and those knick-knacks that mark the living quarters of an English bachelor. There is also an easel with a portrait clamped to it, faced away from the audience. Behind it, on a small table, are various implements of the artist's trade – brushes, pallets, pallet knives, paints, etc.

AT RISE: BASIL HALLWARD, the artist, is standing behind the canvas, painting. His sister, LADY HARRIETT WOTTEN, is sitting on the divan sipping tea. She rises and crosses behind BASIL, and studies the portrait.

HARRIETT
It is your best work, Basil, the best thing you have ever done. You must send it to the Grosvenor. Yes, the Grosvenor is really the only place.

BASIL
It is not finished yet, Harriett. And besides - I don't think I shall send it anywhere.

HARRIETT
(Surprised. Raising an eyebrow.)

Not send it anywhere? My dear fellow, why not? Have you any reason? What odd chaps you Pre-Raphaelites are. You do anything in the world to gain a reputation, and as soon as you have one you throw it all away. It is quite silly of you, for there is only one thing in the world worse than being talked about, and that is not being talked about.

(Studying the portrait.)

Yes, she really is quite exquisite.

BASIL
I know you will laugh at me, but I really can't exhibit it. I've put too much of myself into it.

HARRIETT
(Returns to the divan, sits and laughs.)

Too much of yourself! Upon my word, Basil, I didn't know you were so vain. I really can't see any resemblance between you - with your rugged, strong face - and the sweet, young girl on that canvas. She looks to be all ivory and rose-petals, while you - well, of course you have an intellectual expression and all that - but beauty, true beauty, ends where an intellectual expression begins. Intellect destroys the harmony of a face. The moment one sits down to think one becomes all nose, or all forehead. Look at the successful men in any profession. How perfectly hideous they are! Except of course in the Church. But then in the Church they don't think at all. A bishop at the age of 80 says exactly what he was told when he was 18. As a natural consequence he always looks absolutely delightful.

Who is she?

BASIL
Dorian. Dorian Gray, though I hadn't intended to tell you.

HARRIETT
But why not?

BASIL
Oh, I can't explain it. When I like people immensely, I never tell their names to any one. It is like surrendering a

part of them. I have grown to love secrecy. It is the one thing that can make modern life mysterious. I suppose you think me awfully foolish about it?

HARRIETT
Not at all. You seem to forget that I am married, and the one charm of marriage is that it makes a life of deception absolutely necessary. I never know where my husband is, and my husband never knows what I am doing. When we meet - and we do meet occasionally - we tell each other the most absurd stories with the most serious faces.

BASIL
I hate the way you talk of marriage, Harriett. I believe that you are a very good wife, but that you are thoroughly ashamed of your own virtues. What an extraordinary woman you are. You never say a moral thing, yet you never do anything wrong. Your cynicism is simply a pose.

HARRIETT
Being natural is simply a pose, and the most irritating pose I know. I am afraid I must be going, Basil. But before I go I insist upon your answering my question.

BASIL
What question is that?

HARRIETT
You know perfectly well what question. I want you to explain to me why you won't exhibit your picture of Dorian Gray, and none of this nonsense about revealing yourself. I want the real reason.

BASIL
I told you the real reason, Harriett. Any portrait that is painted with any feeling at all is a portrait of the artist, not of the sitter. The sitter is merely an accident; an occasion. The reason - the real reason - that I will not exhibit this

picture is that I am afraid that I have shown in it the secret of my own soul.

HARRIETT
(Laughing.)

And what is this mysterious secret?

BASIL
I will tell you.

(Pause.)

HARRIETT
(Waiting.)

I am all expectation, Basil.

BASIL
I am afraid you will hardly understand it, and perhaps you will hardly believe it.

HARRIETT
I am quite sure I shall understand it. And as for believing - well, I can believe anything, provided that it is quite incredible.

BASIL
The story is simply this. Two months ago I went to a crush at Lady Brandon's. We of the Pre-Raphaelite Brotherhood must show ourselves in society from time to time, just to remind the public that we are not savages. Put on an evening coat and a white tie and anybody, even a stockbroker, can gain a reputation for being civilized. You told me that yourself.

HARRIETT
(Laughing.)

Yes, I did!

BASIL
Well, after I had been in the room for a few minutes, talking to huge, overdressed dowagers and tedious academians, I suddenly became conscious that someone was looking at me. I turned halfway round and saw Dorian Gray for the first time. Our eyes met. I felt that I had come face to face with someone whose mere personality was so fascinating that, if I allowed it to do so, it would absorb my whole nature, my art, my very soul. Harriett, you know how independent I am by nature. I have always been my own master - at least had always been so... until I met Dorian Gray.

Oh, I don't know how to explain it to you. Something told me I was on the verge of a terrible crisis; that fate had in store for me exquisite joys and exquisite sorrows. I grew afraid and turned to quit the room. It was not conscience that made me do so, Harriett, but cowardice. I take no credit for trying to escape.

HARRIETT
Conscience and cowardice are really the same thing, Basil. Conscience is the trade-name of the firm, that's all.

BASIL
I don't believe that, Harriett, and neither do you. Well, whatever the motive, I stumbled toward the door, and there of course was Lady Brandon.

(Mimicking Lady Brandon's voice.)

You are not going to run away so soon, Mr. Hallward? She screeched out. She has such a curiously shrill voice.

HARRIETT
Yes, she is a peacock in everything but beauty.

BASIL
I couldn't get away from her. She brought me up to Royalties, and people with Stars and Garters, and elderly ladies with gigantic tiaras and parrot noses. And then I found myself face to face with the young woman whose personality had so strangely stirred me. We were quite close, almost touching. It was reckless of me, but I asked Lady Brandon to introduce me to her. Perhaps it was not so reckless, but simply inevitable. We would have spoken to each other even without an introduction. I am sure of that. Dorian told me so afterwards. She, too, felt that we were destined to know each other.

HARRIETT
Lady Brandon treats her guest exactly as an auctioneer treats his goods. She either explains them entirely away, or tells one everything about them except what one wants to know. So tell, me - how did her Ladyship describe this wonderful young lady?

BASIL
Oh, something like,

(Mimicking Lady Brandon's voice.)

'Charming girl – her poor, dear, dead mother and I were absolutely inseparable. Quite forget what she does - afraid she doesn't do anything - oh, yes, plays the piano - or is it the violin?' Neither of us could help laughing, and we became friends at once.

HARRIETT
Laughter is not at all a bad beginning for a friendship, and it is by far the best ending for one.

BASIL
You don't understand what friendship is, Harriett. Or enmity for that matter. You like everyone. That is to say,

you are indifferent to every one.

HARRIETT
How horribly unjust of you. I make a great deal of difference between people. I choose my friends for their good looks, my acquaintances for their good characters, and my enemies for their good intellects. A woman can't be too careful in her choice of enemies. I have not got one who is a fool. They are all people of good intellectual power, and consequently they all appreciate me. Is that very vain of me? I think it is rather vain.

BASIL
I think it is, Harriett. But according to your category, I must be merely an acquaintance.

HARRIETT
My dear Basil, you are much more than an acquaintance, though much less than a friend. What else does one call a brother? But I am not interested in discussing familial relations with you. I like persons better than principles. And I like persons with no principles better than anything else in the world. Now, tell me more about this Dorian Gray. Do you see her often?

BASIL
Every day. I don't think I could be happy if I didn't see her every day. She is absolutely necessary to me.

HARRIETT
How extraordinary! I though you would never care for anything but your art.

BASIL
She is all my art to me now.

HARRIETT
Really? I must meet this Dorian Gray.

BASIL
Harriett, Dorian is to me simply a motive in art. I see everything in her, but you might see nothing at all.

HARRIETT
Then why won't you exhibit her portrait?

BASIL
Because, without intending it, I have put into it some expression of all this curious artistic idolatry. Of course Dorian knows nothing of this and she shall never know anything of it. But the world might guess, and I will not bare my soul to their shallow prying eyes. My heart shall never be up under their microscope. There is too much of myself in the thing, Harriett. Too much!

HARRIETT
Poets are not so scrupulous as you are. At least they know how useful passion is for publication. A broken heart will run for many editions.

BASIL
I hate them for it! An artist should create beautiful things,

but should put nothing of his own life into them. We live in an age when men treat art as if it were a form of autobiography. We have lost the abstract sense of beauty. Some day I will show the world what that means; and for that very reason the world shall never see my picture of Dorian Gray.

HARRIETT
I think you are wrong, Basil, but I won't argue with you. It is only the intellectually lost who ever argue. Tell me, is she fond of you?

BASIL
I think she likes me. I know she likes me. We sit in the studio and talk of a thousand things. Now and then however,

she is horribly thoughtless and seems to take delight in giving me pain. In those moments, Harriett, I feel I have given away my whole soul to someone who treats it as if it were nothing more than a flower for her hair or an ornament for a summer's day.

HARRIETT
Perhaps you will tire sooner than she. One day you will look at her and she will seem to you to be a little out of drawing. Or you won't like her tone of color. You will bitterly reproach her in your own heart and think that she has behaved very badly toward you. The next time she calls, you will be perfectly cold and indifferent. It will be a great pity, for it will alter you.

BASIL
Harriett, don't talk so. As long as I live, the personality of Dorian Gray will dominate me. You can't feel what I feel. You change too often.

HARRIETT
Ah, my dear little brother, that is exactly why I can feel it. Those who are faithful know only the trivial side of love: it is the faithless who know love's tragedies. Why Basil, I have just remembered where I heard the name of Dorian Gray. It was at Aunt Agatha's. She told me she had discovered a wonderful young lady who was going to help her in the East End, and that her name was Dorian Gray. I am bound to state that she never told me she was good looking. Women have no appreciation for good looks. She said that she was very earnest and had a beautiful nature. I immediately assumed her to be a creature with spectacles and lank hair, horribly freckled, and tramping about on huge feet. I wish I had known she was your friend.

BASIL
I'm very glad you didn't.

HARRIETT
Why?

BASIL
I don't want you to meet her.

HARRIETT
You don't want me to meet her?

(PARKER enters.)

PARKER
Miss Dorian Gray to see you, sir.

HARRIETT
(Laughing.)

You must introduce me now.

BASIL
Ask Miss Gray to wait for a few moments and then show her in, Parker.

(PARKER bows and exits.)

Dorian Gray is my dearest friend, Harriett. She has a simple and beautiful nature; Aunt Agatha was quite right. Don't spoil her. Don't try to influence her. Your influence would be bad. The world is wide and has many marvelous people in it for you to corrupt. Don't take away from me the one person who gives to my art whatever charm it possesses; my life as an artist depends on her. Mind, Harriett, I trust you.

HARRIETT
What nonsense you talk.

PARKER
(Enters.)

Miss Dorian Gray.

(Bows and leaves.)

DORIAN
(Enters chattering.)

I am in your Aunt Agatha's black books, Basil. I promised to go to a club in White chapel with her last Tuesday, and I forgot all about it. We were to have played a duet...

(Notices Harriett.)

Oh. Basil. I beg your pardon. I didn't know you had anyone with you.

BASIL
Lady Harriett Wotton; Miss Dorian Gray. Harriett is my *older* sister. I have just been telling her what a capital sitter you were, and now you have spoiled everything.

(Returns to his painting paraphernalia, and prepares to resume working on the portrait.)

HARRIETT
You have not spoiled my pleasure in meeting you, Miss Gray. Our aunt has often spoken to me about you. You are one of her favorites and, I am afraid, one of her victims.

DORIAN
I don't know what she will say to me, now. I am far too frightened to call.

HARRIETT
Oh, I will make your peace with my aunt. She is quite devoted to you. And I don't think it really matters about your not being there. The audience probably thought it was a duet. When Aunt Agatha sits down to the piano, she makes quite enough noise for two people.

DORIAN
(Laughing.)

That is very horrid to her, and not very nice to me.

HARRIETT

You are far too charming to go in for philanthropy, Miss Gray.

BASIL

Harriett, I would like to finish this picture today. Would you think it awfully rude of me if I asked you to go away?

HARRIETT

Am I to go, Miss Gray?

DORIAN

Oh, please don't go, Lady Harriett. I see that Basil is in one of his sulky moods. I can't bear him when he sulks. Besides, I want you to tell me why I should not go in for philanthropy.

HARRIETT

Let us speak of something else, Miss Gray. Philanthropy is so tedious a subject that one would have to talk seriously about it. But since you have asked me to stay…you really don't mind, Basil, do you? You have often told me that you like your sitters to have some one to chat with.

BASIL

(Hesitantly.)

If Dorian wishes it, of course you must stay.

HARRIETT

You are very pressing, Basil, but I am afraid I must go. I have promised to meet a man at the Orleans. Goodbye, Miss Gray. Come and see me some afternoon.

DORIAN

Basil, if Lady Harriett goes I shall go, too. You never say a word while you are painting, and it is horribly dull standing on a platform and trying to look pleasant. Ask her to say. I insist upon it.

BASIL
Do stay, Harriett. She is quite right. I never talk when I am working. And I never listen either. I beg you to stay.

HARRIETT
But what about my man at the Orleans?

BASIL
I don't believe there is any man.

HARRIETT
Quite true. And I do so love it when you beg. Very well. I shall stay.

BASIL
I am forever in your debt. And now, Dorian, stand there and don't move about too much, or pay any attention to my sister. She is a very bad influence on all of her friends and acquaintances with the single exception of myself.

(BASIL begins to paint, quite oblivious to the ensuing conversation.)

DORIAN
Are you really a bad influence, Lady Harriett? As bad as Basil says?

HARRIETT
There is no such thing as a good influence, Miss Gray. All influence is immoral - at least from a scientific point of view.

DORIAN
Why?

HARRIETT
Because if you influence someone, you give them your soul. She no longer thinks her natural thoughts, nor burns with her natural passions. She becomes an echo of someone

else's music, and actor of a part that has not been written for her. Her virtues are no longer real to her; and her sins, if there is such a thing as sin, are borrowed sins. The aim of life is self-development. People are afraid of that so they go in for charity or philanthropy. They feed the hungry, and clothe the beggar, but their own souls starve and are naked. Courage has gone out of our race. Perhaps we never really had it.

BASIL
Just turn your head a little more to the right, Dorian, like a good girl.

HARRIETT
The bravest man among us is afraid of himself. We are punished for our self-denial. The only way to get rid of a temptation is to yield to it. Resist it, and your soul grows sick with longing. Every impulse that we try to strangle broods in the mind and poisons us. The body sins once, and has done with its sin. Nothing remains then but the recollection of a pleasure, or the luxury of a regret. You yourself, Miss Gray, with your rose-red youth and your lily-white girlhood, you have had passions that have made you afraid, daydreams whose mere memory might stain your cheek with shame…"

DORIAN
Stop! Stop, you bewilder me. I don't know what to say. There is some answer to you, but I cannot find it. No, don't speak. Let me think. Or rather, let me try not to think. Basil, I am tired of standing. I must sit down and have a drink of something cool.

BASIL
Dorian, I am so sorry! When I am painting I can think of nothing else. But you were perfect today. I have caught the effect I wanted - the half-parted lips, and the bright look in

the eyes. I don't know what my sister has been saying to you, but it certainly caused you to have the most wonderful expression. I suppose she has been paying you compliments. You mustn't believe a word she says.

DORIAN
She certainly has not been paying me compliments. Perhaps that is the reason I don't believe a word she has told me.

HARRIETT
You know you believe it all. It is horribly hot in here Basil. Do let us have something iced to drink. Something with strawberries in it.

BASIL
Certainly, Harriett. Just touch the bell and when Parker comes tell hem what you want. I can't join you. I have got to finish the background. I have never been in better form for painting than I am today. This is going to be my masterpiece. It is a masterpiece as it stands.

(BASIL returns his attention to the painting while HARRIETT rings the bell. PARKER enters and attends HARRIETT and DORIAN. He leaves and returns shortly with to iced drinks. PARKER exits.)

HARRIETT
Come away from the glare, Miss Gray. You really must not allow yourself to become sunburnt. It would be quite unbecoming and Basil would never paint you again.

DORIAN
(Laughing.)

What can it matter?

HARRIETT
Why, it should matter everything to you, Miss Gray. You have the most marvelous youth, and youth is the one thing

worth having.

DORIAN
I don't feel that way, Lady Harriett.

HARRIETT
No, you don't feel it now. But someday, when you are old and wrinkled; when thought has seared your forehead with its lines, and passion has branded your lips with its hideous fires, you will feel it. It will feel it terribly. Now, where ever you go, you charm the world. Will it always be so? You have a wonderfully beautiful face, Miss Gray. Don't frown at me. You have; and beauty is a form of genius that needs no explanation.

You smile? Ah, when you have lost it you won't smile. The gods have been good to you, Miss Gray. But what the gods give they quickly take away. There is such little time that your youth will last - such a little time, and we never get it back. The pulse of joy that beats in us at twenty becomes sluggish at forty. Our limbs fail, our senses rot. We degenerate into hideous puppets, haunted by the memory of the passions to which we had not the courage to yield.

Ah, Miss Gray, realize your youth while you have it! Don't give away your life to the tedious, the ignorant, the common and the vulgar. These are the sickly alms of our age. Live! Live the wonderful life that is in you! Let nothing be lost upon you. Be always searching for new sensations. Be afraid of nothing. The world belongs to you…but only for a season. Youth! Youth! There is absolutely nothing in the world but youth!

You are glad to have met me, Miss Gray.

DORIAN
Yes, I am glad now. I wonder, shall I always be glad?

HARRIETT
Always! Such a dreadful word, and we women are so fond of using it.

BASIL
Well, it is finished. It is quite finished.

(BASIL steps back. HARRIETT rises to examine his work.)

HARRIETT
My dear little brother, I do congratulate you. It is the finest portrait of modern times. Miss Gray you must come over and look at yourself.

DORIAN
(DORIAN crosses to look at the painting.)

Is it really finished?

BASIL
Quite finished, and you had sat splendidly today.

HARRIETT
That is entirely due to me, isn't it Miss Gray. Miss Gray?

(DORIAN does not answer, but stands as if transfixed by her portrait. There is a moment of silence and then DORIAN suppresses a shiver, and a still says nothing.)

BASIL
Dorian? Don't you like it?

HARRIETT
Of course she likes it. Who wouldn't like it? It is exquisite. I will give you anything you like for it. I must have it.

BASIL
It is not mine to sell, Harriett.

HARRIETT
Whose then?

BASIL
Why, Dorian's, of course.

HARRIETT
Lucky girl.

DORIAN
(Still staring at the painting)

How sad it is. How terribly sad. I shall grow old, and horrible, and dreadful, but this picture will remain forever young. It will never be older than this particular day…if it were only the other way! If only it were I who was to be always young and the picture that was to grow old. For that I would give everything. There is nothing in the wide world I would not give. I would give my soul for that.

(A breeze stirs and a whispered voice says, "Done!" though only DORIAN seems to hear it.)

BASIL
I should object very much to that, Dorian.

DORIAN
(Angry.)

I believe you would, Basil. You like your art better than your friends. I am no more to you than a bronze garden statue. Hardly as much, I dare say. Yes, I am less to you than your ivory Hermes or your silver Faun. You will like them always. How long will you like me? Till I have my first wrinkle, I suppose. Lady Harriett is perfectly right. Youth is the only thing worth having. When I find that I am growing old, I shall kill myself.

BASIL
Dorian, don't talk nonsense. I have never had such a friend as you and I shall never have such another. You are not jealous of material things, are you?

DORIAN
I am jealous of everything whose beauty does not die. I am jealous of the portrait you have painted of me. Why should it keep what I must lose? Every moment that passes takes something from me and gives something to it. Why did you paint it? It will mock me some day - mock me horribly!

(DORIAN crosses to the divan and flings herself down, weeping bitterly.)

BASIL
This is all your fault, Harriett.

HARRIETT
It is the real Dorian Gray.

BASIL
It is not. You should have gone away when I asked.

HARRIETT
I stayed when you asked.

BASIL
Harriett, I cannot quarrel with two people at once. Between the two of you you have made me hate the finest piece of work I have ever done. Fah! I will destroy it. What is it anyway but canvas and color?

(BASIL crosses to the canvas, picks up a pallet knife and prepares to slash the painting.)

DORIAN
(Realizing what BASIL is about to do rises and rushes to him, pulling the knife from his hand.)

No! Basil, don't! It would be murder.

BASIL
Well, I am glad you appreciate my work at last, Dorian.

DORIAN

Appreciate it? I am in love with it, Basil. It is part of me. I feel it.

BASIL

I see. Well then, as soon as you are dry, you shall be varnished, framed and sent home. Then you can do what you like with yourself.

(BASIL walks across to the bell and rings.)

You will have tea, of course, Dorian? And so will you, Harriett? Or do you object to such simple pleasures?

HARRIETT

I adore simple pleasures. They are the last refuge of the complex. But I don't like scenes, except on the stage. How absurd both of you are. I wonder who it was that defined man as a rational animal. It was a most premature definition.

(PARKER appears, BASIL indicates three for tea. He leaves.)

I wish you two would not squabble over the picture. You had much better let me have it, Basil. This silly girl doesn't really want it, and I really do.

DORIAN

If you let any one have it but me, Basil, I shall never forgive you. And I don't allow people to call me a *silly girl*.

BASIL

You know the picture is yours, Dorian. I gave it to you before it existed.

HARRIETT

And you know you have been rather silly, Miss Gray. And I'm sure you don't really object to being reminded that you are extremely young.

DORIAN
I should have objected very strongly this morning, Lady Harriett.

(PARKER enters with a tea-tray.)

PARKER
Shall I pour out, sir?

BASIL
Yes, thank you, Parker.

(As PARKER pours the tea, the conversation continues. When he has served all three he bows slightly to BASIL and wanders to the painting.)

HARRIETT
Ah! This morning! But you have lived since then. Let us all go to the theatre tonight. There is sure to be something on, somewhere.

BASIL
It is such a bore putting on dress clothes. And when one has them on, they feel so horrid.

HARRIETT
Yes, the costume of the 19th century is detestable. It is so somber, so depressing. Sin is the only real color left in modern life.

BASIL
You mustn't say things like that before Dorian, Harriett.

HARRIETT
Before which Dorian? The one who is taking tea with us, or the one in the picture?

BASIL
Before either.

PARKER
It's quite a good likeness, mum, if I'm not getting above myself to say so. It truly captures your soul.

BASIL
Don't touch it, Parker. It has not cured yet.

PARKER
Of course, sir.

(Muttering as he exits.)

It's not like I was born yesterday…

DORIAN
I should like to come to the theatre with you, Lady Harriett.

HARRIETT
Then you shall come; and you will come too, Basil. Won't you?

BASIL
I can't, really. I would sooner not. I have a lot of work to do.

HARRIETT
Well, then, you and I will go it alone Miss Gray.

DORIAN
I should like that awfully.

BASIL
(Indicating the painting)

And I shall stay with the real Dorian Gray.

DORIAN
(Rising and crossing to stare at the portrait again.)

Is that the real Dorian? Am I really like that?

BASIL
Yes, you are exactly like that. At least you are like it in

appearance. But it will never alter. It will remain forever faithful.

HARRIETT
What a fuss people make about fidelity! Why, even in love it is purely a question for physiology. It has nothing whatever to do with our own will. Young men want to be faithful, and are not; old men want to be faithless, and cannot: that is all one can say.

BASIL
Don't go to the theatre tonight, Dorian. Stay and dine with me.

DORIAN
I can't, Basil. I have promised Lady Harriett to go with her.

BASIL
She won't like you any better for keeping your promises. She always breaks her own. I beg you not to go.

(DORIAN shakes her head, no.)

Please.

DORIAN
I must go, Basil.

(BASIL, resigned, sets his tea cup down and walks away.)

BASIL
Very well. It is rather late, and as you have to dress you had better lose no time. Goodbye, Harriett. Goodbye, Dorian. Come and see me soon. Come tomorrow.

DORIAN
Certainly.

BASIL
You won't forget?

DORIAN
No, of course not.

BASIL
And Harriett?

HARRIETT
Yes, Basil?

BASIL
You will remember what I asked you this morning?

HARRIETT
I seem to have forgotten.

BASIL
I trust you.

HARRIETT
Yes. Quite. I wish I could trust myself. Come Miss Gray. My hansom is outside and I can drop you at your own place. Goodbye Basil. It has been a most interesting afternoon.

(HARRIETT and DORIAN exit. BASIL sees them out then returns and stares into the face of his painting.)

(BLACKOUT)

ACT I
Scene 2

SETTING: LORD FERMOR'S study. There are two fine leather chairs separated by an occasional table. Upstage there is an occasional table with a carafe of brandy along with several glasses.

AT RISE: FERMOR is seated, reading. HARRIETT enters.

FERMOR
Well, my loving niece, Harriett. What brings you out so early? I didn't think it fashionable to get out of bed before two, nor to be visible before five.

HARRIETT
Pure family affection, I assure you, Uncle George. I want to get something out of you.

FERMOR
Money, I suppose. Well, sit down and tell me all about it. Young people nowadays imagine that money is everything.

HARRIETT
(Leaning over to kiss him on the forehead.)

Yes, and when they grow older they know it is.

(She settles herself in a chair opposite FERMOR.)

But I don't want money, Uncle George. It is only people who pay their bills who want money, and I never pay mine. Credit is the capital of the younger generation, and one lives charmingly upon it. No, what I want is information.

FERMOR
Well, I can tell you anything that is in an English Blue-Book, Harriett, although those fellows nowadays write a lot of nonsense. When I was in the Diplomatic, things were much better. But nowadays I hear they let them in by examination. What can you expect? Examinations are pure humbug from beginning to end. If a man is a gentleman, he knows quite enough. And if he is not a gentleman, whatever he knows is bad for him.

HARRIETT
Miss Dorian Gray does not belong to Blue-Books, Uncle.

FERMOR
Really? Dorian Gray, you say? Who is she?

HARRIETT
That is what I have come to learn, Uncle. Or rather, I know who she is. She is the last Lord Kelso's granddaughter. Her mother was a Devereaux; Lady Margaret Devereaux. I want you to tell me about her mother. What was she like? Whom did she marry? You have known nearly everybody in your time, so you might have known her.

FERMOR
Kelso's granddaughter? Kelso's granddaughter! Of course! I believe I was at her christening. Extraordinarily beautiful girl, Margaret Devereaux. Made all the men frantic by running away with a penniless young fellow; a nobody; a subaltern in a foot regiment or some such nonsense like that. Poor chap was killed in a dual a few months after the marriage. Ugly story about it. Remember it like it was yesterday. They say old Kelso got some rascally adventurer to insult his son-in-law in public. Paid him to do it. Paid him, I say. Big fellow spitted him like he was a Christmas goose.

Oh, it was all hushed up, but, egad, Kelso ate his chop alone at the club for some time after that. Brought his daughter back home with him, I was told. But she never spoke to him again. Bad business, that. She died, too. Within the year. Had a daughter, did she? I say. I had forgotten that. What sort of girl is she? Pretty thing if she's anything like her mother.

HARRIETT
(Rises and crosses to the table with the brandy and pours herself a glass. She returns to her chair.)

Quite pretty. Would you care for some brandy?

FERMOR
Bit early in the day for me, I'm afraid. She should have a pot of money waiting for her if Kelso did right by her. Her mother had money, too. All the Selby property came to her through her maternal grandfather. He hated Kelso; thought him a mean dog. He was, too. Came to Madrid once when I was there. Egad, I was ashamed of him....

HARRIETT
Yes, yes, I'm sure. She has Selby, I knew that, but she hasn't come of age yet. Her mother... she was very beautiful?

FERMOR
Margaret Devereaux was one of the loveliest creatures I ever saw, Harriett. What on earth induced her to behave as she did, I never could understand. She could have married anybody she chose. Carlington was mad after her. She was romantic, though. All the women in that family were. The men were a poor lot, but egad, the women were lovely.

By the way, Harriett, talking about silly marriages, what is this humbug your father tells me about Dartmoor wanting to marry an American? Ain't English girls good enough for him?

HARRIETT
It is rather fashionable to marry Americans just now, Uncle George.

FERMOR
I'll back English women against the world, Harriett. American women don't last.

HARRIETT
A long engagement exhausts them, but they are capital at a steeplechase. They take things flying. I don't think Dartmoor has a chance.

FERMOR
But who are her people? Has she got any?

HARRIETT
American girls are as clever at concealing their parents as English women are at concealing their past.

FERMOR
Pork packers, I suppose?

HARRIETT
I do hope so, Uncle, for Dartmoor's sake. I am told that pork packing is the most lucrative profession in America…after politics.

FERMOR
Is she pretty?

HARRIETT
She behaves as if she were beautiful. Most American women do. It is the secret of their charm.

FERMOR
Why can't these American women stay in their own

country? They are always telling us that it is the paradise for women.

HARRIETT
It is. That is the reason why, like Eve, they are so excessively anxious to get out of it.

(She rises to leave.)

Goodbye, Uncle George. I shall be late for lunch if I stay any longer.

(BLACKOUT)

ACT I
Scene 3

SETTING: One month later. LADY HARRIETT'S home.

AT RISING: DORIAN is seated, waiting for HARRIETT, who is, of course, late. HARRIETT enters accompanied by LADY MARGUERITE DE NAVARRE.)

DORIAN
How late you are, Harriett.

HARRIETT
So sorry, Dorian. I went to look after a piece of old brocade in Wardour Street and had to bargain for hours for it. Nowadays people know the price of everything and the value of nothing. Of course you know Lady Marguerite de Navarre?

DORIAN
I've not had the pleasure.

HARRIETT
Lady Marguerite - Miss Dorian Gray.

MARGUERITE
Charmed.

HARRIETT
I lunched with Victor today. He is a sentimental man. Never marry a sentimental man, Dorian.

DORIAN
But I like sentimental men.

HARRIETT
Never marry at all. Men marry because they are tired;

women because they are curious. Both are disappointed. Just ask Marguerite. When her third husband died, her hair turned quite gold from grief.

DORIAN
Harriett! How can you say such a thing?

MARGUERITE
Pay no attention to Harriett, Miss Gray. She is really wonderful, and so full of surprises. But she is still décolleté. When she wears one of her smart gowns she looks like an *edition deluxe* of a bad French novel.

HARRIETT
And yet Marguerite is the one with the prodigious capacity for familial affection. After all, Ferrol is her fourth husband, and I am still working on my first. I hear she had all their hearts embalmed and hung at her girdle.

MARGUERITE
You mustn't believe a word of it, Miss Gray. It is all nonsense, for none of my husbands had any heart at all.

DORIAN
Lady Marguerite, if it is not too forward of me to ask, you are so young and beautiful. Why do you marry such old men who seem to die so frequently?

MARGUERITE
My dear, old men are delightful. They require so little while they are alive, and they leave so much behind when they die.

DORIAN
I don't think I am likely to marry, Harriett. I am too much in love for that.

HARRIETT
In love, you say? With who?

DORIAN
With an actor.

MARGUERITE
That is a rather common debut.

DORIAN
You would not say so if you saw him, Lady Marguerite. John Vane.

MARGUERITE
Never heard of him.

DORIAN
No one has. People will someday, however. He is a genius.

MARGUERITE
My dear, no man is a genius. Men are a decorative sex. They never have anything to say, but they say it so charmingly.

HARRIETT
Quite true. Ultimately there are only two kinds of men - the plain kind and the fancy kind. Plain men are useful if you want to gain a reputation for respectability. Fancy men are very charming but they can't be admitted into decent society. But enough of that. Tell us about your genius. Is he plain or fancy? How long have you know him?

DORIAN
About three weeks, and you mustn't be unsympathetic about it. After all, it never would have happened if I had not met you. You filled me with the wild desire to know everything about life.

I remember you once said the search for beauty was the real secret of life. So I went in search of beauty, and I found it at this little theatre. I paid a whole guinea for a stage box - I can't tell you to this day why I did so. Yet, if I hadn't I should have missed the greatest romance of my life.

I see you are laughing at me. It is horrid of you.

HARRIETT
We are not laughing, Dorian. At least not at you. But you should not say the greatest romance of you life. You should say the first romance of your life. This is merely the beginning.

DORIAN
Do you think my nature is so shallow?

HARRIETT
No. I think your nature is so deep. People who love only once in their lives are really the shallow people. What they call loyalty, I call lethargy. But don't let me interrupt you. Go on with your story.

DORIAN
Well, I found myself seated in a horrid little private box, with a vulgar drop-scene staring me in the face. Women went about selling oranges and ginger-beer, and there was a terrible consumption of nuts going on. I began to wonder what on earth I should do when I caught sight of the play-bill. What do you think the play was?

MARGUERITE
I should think *The Idiot Boy* or *Dumb but Innocent*. Our fathers used to like that sort of thing. The longer I live the more keenly I feel that whatever was good enough for our fathers in not good enough for us.

DORIAN
This play was good enough for us, Lady Marguerite. It was Romeo and Juliet. I must admit I was rather annoyed at the idea of seeing Shakespeare done in such a wretched hole of a place. But I was determined to wait through the first act. Mercutio was a stout, elderly gentleman, with a husky voice

and a figure like a beer-barrel, and Juliet was a slip of a girl, all coiffed and painted.

But then Romeo appeared with a face like the sun and dark brown hair, eyes that were violet wells of passion, lips like the petals of a rose - he was the loveliest thing I have ever seen in my life. And his voice...!

Ordinary men, whether fancy or plain, never appeal to one's imagination. No glamour ever transfigures them. There is no mystery in any of them. But how different an actor is!

Harriett, why didn't you tell me that the only thing worth loving is an actor?

HARRIETT
Because I have loved so many of them, Dorian. But what are your actual relations with this actor, this...John Vane?

DORIAN
Harriett, John Vane is sacred!

HARRIETT
Of course he is. It is only the sacred things that are worth touching. I suppose he must belong to you someday. When one is in love, one always begins by deceiving one's self, and one always ends by deceiving others. That is what the world calls a romance. You have, at least, met him?

DORIAN
Of course I have met him. That first night at the theatre, the house manager, a Mr. Isaacs, offered to take me behind the scenes and introduce me to him. John was so shy and so gentle. There is something of a child about him. His eyes opened wide in exquisite wonder when I told him what I thought of his performance. I think we were both rather nervous. Mr. Isaacs insisted on calling my 'my lady,' but John said, 'Surely not a lady, but a princess.'

MARGUERITE
Upon my word, Harriett, this Mr. Vane knows how to pay a compliment.

DORIAN
From the top of his head to the toe of his shoes he is entirely divine. I've gone to see him act every night since, and every night he is more marvelous.

HARRIETT
This is the reason, I suppose, that you never dine with me now. I thought you must have some curious romance on hand, though this is not quite what I had expected.

DORIAN
I can't help going to see John act. I am hungry for his presence.

HARRIETT
Well, you can make it up to me by dining with us tonight.

DORIAN
Tonight he is Henry V, and tomorrow, Orlando.

MARGUERITE
When is he John Vane?

DORIAN
Never.

MARGUERITE
Oh, good! I congratulate you.

DORIAN
How horrid you both are! I tell you he has genius. I love him. And I must make him love me. Harriett, you know all the secrets of life. Tell me how to charm John Vane. I want to make Juliet jealous. I want the dead lovers of the world to hear our laughter and grow sad. I want a breath of our

passion to stir their dust into consciousness, to wake their ashes into pain. Harriett, how I worship him.

HARRIETT
And just what is it you propose to do, now?

DORIAN
I want you and Basil to come with me to the theatre. You must come, too, Lady Marguerite. I want all of society to acknowledge his genius.

HARRIETT
Very well. What night shall we go?

DORIAN
Tonight!

MARGUERITE
Impossible.

DORIAN
Thursday, then. He plays Romeo on Thursday. Let us fix Thursday.

HARRIETT
All right. The Bristol at eight o'clock; and I will get Basil.

DORIAN
Not eight, Harriett. Please. Half-past six. We must be there before the curtain rises. You must see him in the first act when he meets Juliet.

MARGUERITE
Half-past six! What an hour! No one dines before seven.

(BLACKOUT)

ACT I
Scene 4

SETTING: Dressing room of JOHN VANE. It is sparse, with a dressing table, a chair, and theatrical paraphernalia such as masks, make-up, a sword, etc.

AT RISE: JOHN is pacing. His mother, MRS. VANE, is seated.

JOHN
Mother, are you not happy for me?

MRS. VANE
Happy? I am only happy when I see you act. You must think of nothing but your acting. Mr. Isaacs has been very good to us, and we owe him money.

JOHN
Money, Mother? What does money matter? Love is more important than money.

MRS. VANE
Mr. Isaacs has advanced us fifty pounds to pay off our debts and to get a proper education for Sibyl. You must not forget that, John. Fifty pounds is a very large sum of money. Mr. Isaacs has been most considerate.

JOHN
He is no gentleman, Mother. And I hate the way he looks at you.

MRS. VANE
I don't know how we could manage without him.

JOHN
We won't need him anymore, Mother, once Dorian and I are wed.

MRS. VANE
Foolish child. Foolish, foolish child!

JOHN
Foolish I may be, Mother. But I love her. And she loves me, without thought of her station or mine. She does not make me feel humbled by her love. No, I feel proud, terribly proud. Mother, don't look so sad. Please, Mother. Let me be in love!

MRS. VANE
My child, you are far too young to think of falling in love. Besides, what do you know of this Dorian Gray? The whole thing is most inconvenient. I would think you would have more consideration. Of course…if she really is rich…

JOHN
Oh, Mother…

(SIBYL VANE, JOHN's young sister, enters the room. She walks dutifully to her mother and kisses her on the cheek.)

JOHN
You might keep some of your kisses for me, Sibyl.

SIBYL
Ah, but you don't like being kissed, John. You are a dreadful old bear.

(SIBYL runs across the room and hugs him.)

I hear there is a strange woman who comes to the theatre every night and comes backstage to talk.

JOHN
You have been listening where you ought not to be.

SIBYL
Does she love you?

JOHN
What a question is that for a young girl?

SIBYL
You didn't answer. Don't you know if she loves you?

JOHN
I believe her attachment to me is quite sincere. I also believe she is quite possibly a member of the aristocracy. I see no reason why we should not contract an alliance. It might even be a most brilliant marriage.

SIBYL
It is clear that you are mad for her, but does she love you?

JOHN
Dear Sibyl, you talk as if you were a hundred. Someday you will be in love yourself. Then you will know what it is. Don't look sulky. Surely you should be happy for me. I am quite happier than I have ever been. I shall love her forever.

SIBYL
And she, too?

JOHN
Forever, too.

SIBYL
She had better. For as sure as there is a God in heaven, if she ever does you any wrong, I shall kill her.

(BLACKOUT)

ACT I
Scene 5

SETTING: BASIL'S studio. It has not changed other than there is now no painting paraphernalia.

AT RISE: BASIL and MARGUERITE are seated as PARKER shows HARRIETT in.

HARRIETT
I suppose you have heard the news?

MARGUERITE
No, Harriett. What is it? Nothing about politics I hope.

HARRIETT
Dorian Gray is engaged to be married.

BASIL
Dorian, engaged? Impossible!

HARRIETT
It is perfectly true.

BASIL
To whom?

HARRIETT
To some actor or other.

BASIL
I can't believe it. Dorian is far too sensible to do something so foolish.

HARRIETT
Dorian is far too wise not to do something foolish now and again.

BASIL

Marriage is hardly a thing that one can do now and again, Harriett.

MARGUERITE

Except in America.

HARRIETT

But I didn't say she was married. I said she was engaged to be married. There is a great difference.

BASIL

But think of Dorian's birth; her position and wealth. It would be absurd for her to marry so much beneath her.

HARRIETT

If you want to make her marry this actor, you tell her just that, Basil. She is sure to do it, then.

MARGUERITE

I do hope he is a good fellow, Harriett. I don't want to see Dorian tied to some vile creature who might degrade her nature and ruin her intellect.

HARRIETT

Dorian says he is both good and handsome, and she is not often wrong about things of that kind. Basil's portrait of her has quickened her appreciation for the personal appearance of others. We are to see him tonight at the theatre.

MARGUERITE

But do you approve of it Harriett? You can't possibly approve. It is a silly infatuation.

HARRIETT

I never approve or disapprove of anything, Marguerite. You know that. It is an absurd attitude to take towards life. Besides, every experience is of value, and whatever one may say against marriage, it is certainly an experience. I hope Dorian will marry this actor, passionately adore him for six months or so, and then suddenly become fascinated by someone else. That would be a wonderful study.

BASIL
You don't mean a word of all that, Harriett. You know you don't. If Dorian's life were spoiled, no one would be sorrier than you.

HARRIETT
No life is spoiled but one whose growth is arrested. As for marriage, of course that would be silly. There are other and far more interesting bonds between men and women. Marriage does, however, have the charm of being fashionable.

(PARKER ushers DORIAN into the room.)

But here is Dorian. She can certainly tell you more about all this than I can.

DORIAN
My dear Harriett. My dear Basil. Lady Marguerite. You must all congratulate me! I have never been so happy. Of course it is sudden, but all really delightful things are. And yet it seems to me to be the one thing I have been looking for all my life.

BASIL
I hope you will always be very happy, Dorian. But I don't quite forgive you for not having let me know of your engagement. You let Harriett know.

MARGUERITE
What I can't forgive is being late for dinner. Come, let us go. We must try out this new chef, and then you will tell us how it all came about.

DORIAN
But there is not much to tell, and I can't wait to tell it. What

happened was simply this. Yesterday I went down to the theatre. John was playing Orlando. When the performance was over, I went behind and spoke with him. As we were sitting together, there came into his eyes a look I had never seen before. My lips moved toward his…and we kissed. I can't describe to you what I felt at that moment. It seemed that all my life had been narrowed to one perfect point of rose-coloured joy.

HARRIETT
Dorian, at what particular point did the word, 'Marriage,' come up? He did *ask* you to marry him? You did say, 'Yes?'

DORIAN
I did not treat it as a business transaction, if that is what you mean. And he did not make a formal proposal. But he told me that he loved me - that he was not worthy to be my husband. Not worthy! Why, the whole world is nothing to me compared to him.

HARRIETT
Men are wonderfully practical; much more practical than we are. In situations of this kind they often forget to say anything about marriage and we always remind them.

BASIL
Don't, Harriett. You are annoying Dorian. She is not like other women. She would never bring misery upon anyone.

HARRIETT
Dorian is never annoyed with me. And I asked the question for the best reason possible - simple curiosity.

DORIAN
You are quite insufferable, Harriett; but I don't mind. It is impossible to be angry with you. I love John Vane. I want to put him on a pedestal of gold and worship at his feet. His trust makes me faithful. His belief makes me good. When I

am with him, I regret all that you have taught me. The slightest touch of John's hand makes me forget you and all your wrong, fascinating, poisonous, delightful theories.

HARRIETT
Pleasure is the only thing worth having a theory about. But I am afraid I cannot claim it as my own. It belongs to nature, not to me. Pleasure is nature's sign of approval. When we are happy, we are always good. But when we are good, we are not always happy.

DORIAN
But what do you mean by 'good?'

MARGUERITE
To be good is to be in harmony with one's self; one's own life - that is the important thing. Individualism is the higher aim.

BASIL
But surely, if one lives merely for one's self, one pays a terrible price for doing so.

HARRIETT
Yes, we are overcharged for everything nowadays. The real tragedy of the poor is that they can afford nothing more than self-denial. Beautiful sins are the privilege of the rich.

BASIL
We pay for our sins with more than money, Harriett. We pay in remorse, in suffering, in the consciousness of degradation.

HARRIETT
My dear little brother, Medieval art is charming, but Medieval emotions are out of date. Believe me, no civilized man ever regrets pleasure, and no uncivilized man ever even knows what pleasure is.

DORIAN
I know what pleasure is. It is to adore someone.

MARGUERITE
Well, that is certainly better than being adored. Being adored is a nuisance. Men treat us just as humanity treats its gods. They worship us and are always bothering us to do something for them.

DORIAN
I should have said men create love in our natures and have a right to demand it back.

BASIL
Here, here! That is quite true, Dorian.

HARRIETT
Nothing is ever *quite* true.

DORIAN
But you must admit that men give women the very gold of their lives.

HARRIETT
Possibly. But they invariably want it back in such very small change.

DORIAN
Harriett, you are dreadful. I don't like you at all.

HARRIETT
You will always like me, Dorian. I represent to you all the sins you have never had the courage to commit.

DORIAN
What nonsense you talk. Come, let us go to down to the theatre. When John comes on stage you will have a new ideal of life.

(BLACKOUT)

ACT I
Scene 6

SETTING: A dingy box of a dingy theatre.

AT RISE: DORIAN, HARRIETT, MARGUERITE, and BASIL enter and sit down. There is much chatter from the lower class audience on the orchestra level below.

HARRIETT
What a place to find one's divinity in!

DORIAN
Yes. It was here that I found him, and he is divine. When he acts, you forget everything. The common people with their coarse faces and rough ways sit silently and watch. They weep and laugh as he wills them to. He spiritualizes them, and one feels that they are of the same flesh and blood as one's self.

MARGUERITE
The same flesh and blood as one's self?! Oh, I should hope not.

BASIL
Pay her no mind, Dorian. I understand exactly what you mean. Any any man who has the effect you describe must be fine and noble. If this young man can give a soul to those who have lived without one, then he is worthy of all your adoration. This marriage is quite right. I did not think so at first. I admit that now. But I believe you must have been made for each other.

DORIAN
Thank you, Basil. I knew you would understand. Look, the

curtain is about to rise, and you will see the man to whom I am going to give all of my life.

(Lights dim as we hear JOHN VANE as Romeo in voice over. Lights rise.)

JOHN (in voice over)
O, she doth teach the torches to burn bright!
It seems she hangs upon the cheek of night
Like a rich jewel in an Ethiope's ear;
Beauty too rich for use, for earth too dear!
So shows a snowy dove trooping with crows,
As yonder lady o'er her fellows shows.
The measure done, I'll watch her place of stand,
And, touching hers, make blessed my rude hand.
Did my heart love till now? forswear it, sight!
For I ne'er saw true beauty till this night.

(While most of the actors are passable, JOHN VANE's performance is wooden, joyless, and curiously listless. The crowd responds with boos and hisses. As the play progresses DORIAN becomes more embarrassed and angry. DORIAN, BASIL, MARGUERITE, and HARRIETT continue their conversation over the play.)

MARGUERITE
He is lovely to gaze upon, Dorian, but he can't act. Let us go. I am quite famished.

DORIAN
No. Do go on without me. I am going to see the play through. I am awfully sorry that I have made you waste an evening. I apologize to you all.

BASIL
Dorian, I should think Mr. Vane was ill. We will come again some other night.

DORIAN

I wish he were ill. But he seems to me to be simply callous and cold. He is entirely altered. Last night he was a great artist. This evening he is merely a commonplace, mediocre actor.

BASIL

Don't talk like that about someone you love, Dorian. Love is a more wonderful thing than Art.

MARGUERITE

They are both simply forms of imitation. But do let us go. Dorian, you must not stay here any longer. It is not good for one's morals to see bad acting. Besides, I don't suppose you would allow your husband to act on the stage, so what does it matter if he plays Romeo like a wooden doll? He is handsome, and if he knows as little about life as he knows about acting, he will be a delightful experience.

HARRIETT

Oh, good heavens, girl. Don't look so tragic. The secret of remaining young is never to have an emotion that is unbecoming. Come to the restaurant with us. We will smoke cigarettes and drink to the beauty of John Vane. He is beautiful. What more can you want?

DORIAN

Go away, Harriett. You too, Basil. Please, all of you, just go.

(HARRIETT, MARGUERITE, and BASIL exit. DORIAN broods as the play continues. The lights slowly fade to black.)

(BLACKOUT)

ACT I

Scene 7

SETTING: JOHN VANE'S dressing room.

AT RISE: JOHN is standing alone, triumphant, waiting for DORIAN to come. He laughs at some secret joke. DORIAN enters. She is obviously furious, but JOHN doesn't recognize it at first.

JOHN
How badly I acted tonight, Dorian!

DORIAN
Horribly.

JOHN
(Suddenly realizing that something is terribly wrong.)

Dorian?

DORIAN
How could you? You were horrible; dreadful. You have no idea what I suffered tonight.

JOHN
Dorian, you should have understood. But, you understand now - don't you?

DORIAN
Understand what?

JOHN
Why I acted so badly tonight. Why I shall always be bad. Why I shall never act well again.

DORIAN
I suppose you are ill. When you are ill you shouldn't act. You make yourself ridiculous. My friends were with me tonight. My friends were bored. I was bored.

JOHN
Oh Dorian, Dorian, before I knew you, acting was the one reality in my life. It was only in the theatre that I lived. I thought that it was all true. I was Caesar one night, and Richard the next. The joy of Romeo was mine, as was the sorrow of Othello. I believed it. I believed it all. The painted scenes were my world. I knew nothing but shadows and thought them real.

Then you came, my beautiful love, and you freed my soul from prison. You taught me what reality is. Tonight, for the first time in my life, I saw through the hollowness of the empty pageant in which I had always played. The words were not my words. They were but a reflection of something grander, and higher. You made me understand what love is. Dorian, I am sick of shadows. I hate the stage, for though I might mimic a passion that I do not feel, I cannot mimic the one that burns in my soul like fire. Oh Dorian, don't you understand? Even if I could, it would be profane for me to play at being in love.

DORIAN
(Unmoved.)

You have killed my love.

JOHN
Dorian, you don't mean that.

 (JOHN Crosses to DORIAN, takes her hand and presses it to his lips. She pulls way.)

DORIAN
Yes. You have killed my love. You used to stir my

imagination, but now you don't even stir my curiosity. I loved you because you had genius and intellect, because you realized the dreams of great poets and gave shape and substance to the shadows of art. You have thrown it all away. What a fool I have been. I was mad to love you. You are nothing to me now.

JOHN
You are not serious, Dorian? You are acting.

DORIAN
Acting? I leave that to you. You do it so well.

(DORIAN turns to go. JOHN reaches for her arm, turning her towards him. DORIAN slaps him hard.)

Don't touch me. I am going.

JOHN
Dorian! Dorian, don't leave me. I am sorry I didn't act well. I was thinking of you the whole time. My love for you came over me so suddenly. I think I should never have known it if you had not kissed me - if we had not kissed each other. Kiss me again, my love. Don't go away. Please, can't you forgive me?

DORIAN
I don't wish to be unkind, but I can't see you again. You have disappointed me.

(DORIAN exits. JOHN watches incredulously, sinks to his knees weeping.)

(BLACKOUT)

ACT I
Scene 8

SETTING: DORIAN'S home, later that night. The room is elegant. There is a desk with writing implements on it. There is a sofa, a chair, and The Picture of DORIAN GRAY hanging on the wall. The picture has altered from its original state. It now shows DORIAN with a cruel and angry look on her face.

AT RISE: DORIAN is, pacing, talking out loud to herself.

DORIAN
I was not cruel. It was all his fault. He pretended to be a great artist, but he was nothing but a third rate actor with a pretty face. He made me love him and then he disappointed me. It was his fault. He was shallow and unworthy.

(She glances at the portrait and frowns as if something is wrong. She rises and continues talking as she crosses, talking to the portrait.)

I suffered too. During the three hours of that horrible play I lived centuries of pain, eons of humiliation. Why should I trouble myself about John Vane? He is nothing to me now.

(She begins to examine the picture. It is definitely different. The face now has a cruel set to its mouth, and wanton look in its gaze. DORIAN continues to talk to the portrait.)

It is impossible. You can't have changed. It is folly to think so.

DORIAN (V.O.)
If only it were I who was to be always young and the picture that was to grow old. For that I would give everything.

There is nothing in the wide world I would not give. I would give my soul for that.

DORIAN

And yet, you have. How cruel the set of you mouth. You have altered already, and will alter more. Your gold will wither to gray; your red and white roses will die. For every sin I commit, a stain will fleck your features and wreck your fairness. You will be to me, changed or unchanged, a visible emblem of conscience.

(DORIAN turns away.)

But I will not sin. I will resist temptation. It is all Harriett's fault with her poisonous theories. I'll not see her again. I'll go back to John and make amends. I will marry him and we will be happy together. Life will be beautiful and pure.

(DORIAN turns back to the picture, reaches out her hand to touch its face.)

How horrible.

(BLACKOUT)

ACT II

Scene 1

SETTING: The following day. The home of DORIAN GRAY.

AT RISE: DORIAN enters the room and sits at her desk. Her maid, ALICE, sets breakfast for her.

ALICE
You've slept well, my lady.

DORIAN
What o'clock is it, Alice?

ALICE
Quarter past one, mum.

(DORIAN sits to her breakfast. Her eyes fall on her portrait and she shudders.)

ALICE
Too cold for you, mum? I'll just shut the window.

DORIAN
No. Thank you. I am not cold. And I am not hungry. You may take this and go, Alice.

(ALICE clears the dishes and begins to exit.)

And Alice. I am not at home…to anyone.

ALICE
Yes, mum.

(DORIAN paces for a moment, steels herself, and then faces the canvas.)

DORIAN
It's true. Perfectly true. I didn't imagine it or dream it. The

portrait has altered. Can that truly be the image of my soul? And if it is, why? Those lips, so cruel. Are you what I am inside? You are, aren't you, a visible symbol of the degradation of sin in my soul. I know what I must do. I shall go to John and confess my sin, for it is the confession, not the priest that grants absolution.

(There is an insistent knocking on his door, followed by HARRIETT's voice.)

HARRIETT (From offstage)
Dorian. Dorian, I must see you. Let me in at once. I can't bear you shutting yourself up like this.

(DORIAN takes a moment to draw a screen in front of the portrait before opening the door. HARRIETT enters and embraces DORIAN.)

Oh, Dorian, I am so sorry for it all. But you must not think too much about it.

DORIAN
You mean about John?

HARRIETT
Yes, of course, about John. It is dreadful, from one point of view, but it was not your fault. Tell me, did you go backstage and see him, after the play was over?

DORIAN
Yes.

HARRIETT
I felt sure you had. Did you make quite a scene?

DORIAN
I was brutal, Harriett. Perfectly brutal. But it is all right now. I am not sorry for anything that has happened. It has taught me to know myself better.

HARRIETT

Ah, Dorian. I am so glad you take it that way. I was afraid I would find you plunged in remorse, and tearing out that lovely hair of yours.

DORIAN

I have got through all that. I am perfectly happy now. To begin with, I know what conscience is, and it is not what you told me it was. It is the divinest thing in us. Don't sneer at me Harriett. I want to be good. I can't bear the idea of my soul being hideous.

HARRIETT

A very charming basis for ethics, Dorian. I congratulate you on it. But how are you going to begin?

DORIAN

By marrying John Vane.

HARRIETT

Marrying…But Dorian…

DORIAN

I know what you are going to say, Harriett. Something dreadful about marriage. Well don't say it. Two days ago John Vane asked me to marry him and I am going to be his wife.

HARRIETT

Dorian…dear…didn't you get my letter? I wrote to you this morning, and sent the note down by my own man.

DORIAN

Your letter? Oh, yes, I remember. I have not read it yet, Harriett. I was afraid there might be something in it that I wouldn't like. You cut life to pieces with your epigrams.

HARRIETT

Then you don't know.

DORIAN
What do you mean?

HARRIETT
(Crossing to DORIAN and taking her hands.)

Dorian, my letter was to tell you…John Vane is dead.

DORIAN
Dead? John dead? It is not true! It is a horrible lie. How dare you say it?

HARRIETT
It is quite true, Dorian. It is in all the morning papers. I wrote to you to ask you not to see any one till I came. There is to be an inquest, of course, and you must not be mixed up in it. Things like that make a woman fashionable in Paris, but in London people are so prejudiced.

DORIAN
Harriett, did you say an inquest? What did you mean by that? Did John…Oh, Harriett, I can't bear it. Be quick. Tell me everything at once.

HARRIETT
It was no accident, Dorian. It seems that as he was leaving the theatre with his mother, he said he had forgotten something upstairs. She waited for him for sometime, but he didn't come back down. They found him lying dead on the floor of his dressing room. He had swallowed something dreadful that they use in the theatre - I don't know what it was, but it had either prussic acid or white lead in it. He seems to have died instantaneously.

DORIAN
Harriett, Harriett, this is terrible!

HARRIETT
Yes, very tragic. But you must not get yourself mixed up in

it. And you mustn't let this thing get on your nerves. I'll tell you what - you must come and dine with me. Afterwards we will look in at the opera.

DORIAN
So I have murdered John Vane; murdered him as surely as if I had cut his throat with a knife. Can they feel, I wonder, those silent people we call the dead? John? Can he feel, or know, or listen? Oh, Harriett, how I loved him once. It seems years ago now. Was it really only last night that he played so badly and broke my heart? I hurt him terribly, Harriett. Something happened last night that made me afraid. I can't tell you what it is, but it was terrible. I felt that I had done wrong and I was determined to go back to him and make things right, and now he is dead.

Harriett, what shall I do? You don't know the danger my soul is in, and there is nothing to keep me straight. He would have done that for me. He had no right to kill himself. It was selfish of him. Terribly selfish.

HARRIETT
Dorian, if you had married this man, you would have been wretched. Of course you would have treated him kindly. One can always be kind to people about whom one cares nothing about. But he would have soon found out that you were absolutely indifferent to him. I say nothing about the social mistake, which would have been abject. I assure you the whole thing would have been an absolute failure.

DORIAN
I suppose it would. But I thought it my duty. It is not my fault that this terrible tragedy has prevented me doing what was right. Harriett, why is it that I cannot feel this tragedy as much as I want to? I don't think I am heartless. Do you?

HARRIETT
You have done too many foolish things during the last

fortnight to be entitled to that description, Dorian.

DORIAN
I'm not sure I like your explanation, Harriett, but I am glad you don't think I am heartless. I am nothing of the kind. I know I am not.

HARRIETT
Sometimes a tragedy that possesses artistic elements of beauty crosses our lives. In the present case, what has really happened? Some one has killed himself for love of you. I wish that I had ever had such an experience. It would have made me in love with love for the rest of my life.

DORIAN
I was terribly cruel to him. You forget that.

HARRIETT
I am sure you were splendid. I have never seen you really and absolutely angry. Do you remember how you told me that John Vane came to life when he was on the stage?

DORIAN
He will never come to life again.

HARRIETT
No, he will never come to life again. He has played his last part. But, Dorian, the young man never really lived, and so he never really died. To you at least he was always a dream - a phantom that flitted through Shakespeare's plays and left them lovelier for his presence. The moment he touch real life, he marred it. And it marred him. Mourn for Romeo if you like. Put ashes on your head because Hamlet was poisoned. Cry out against heaven because McBeth murdered sleep. But don't waste your tears on John Vane. He was less real than they are.

(There is a brief silence between the two.)

DORIAN
You have explained me to myself, Harriett. I felt all that you said, but was afraid of it, and could not express it myself. We will not talk of this again. It has been a marvelous experience. That is all. I wonder if life has still in store for me anything as marvelous. I think I shall join you at the opera, Harriett, but I feel too tired to eat.

HARRIETT
Goodbye then, Dorian. I shall see you before nine-thirty.

(HARRIETT exits. DORIAN waits for a moment and then takes the screen from in front of the portrait and examines it.)

DORIAN
You received the news of John's death before I, didn't you. The cruelty that mars your lovely mouth no doubt appeared the very moment he drank the poison. I wonder, do you respond to results of my actions, or are you merely cognizant of what transpires within my soul? It would be fascinating if I could one day watch the transformation take place right before my very eyes.

(She wanders around the room.)

Poor John. He often mimicked death on stage. I wonder how he played out that last, dreadful scene? Did he curse me as he died? No, I think not. He died for love of me. Oh, John, I did love you. I shall forever remember you as a wonderful, tragic figure sent on to the world's stage to show the supreme reality of love.

(Walking back toward the portrait, addressing it.)

But now it is time to live, and what does life hold for me? Eternal youth? Infinite passion? Pleasures subtle and secret, wild joys and wilder sins? Am I to have all these things while you bear the burden of my shame? You changed in answer to a wild, foolish prayer. Perhaps in answer to another prayer you might remain unchanged. But then, to be forever young? Who would surrender that chance, what ever the consequences might be?

No, I'll never again tempt by prayer any terrible power. If you are to alter, you will alter. That is all. Indeed, it will be a pleasure to watch you. You will be the most magical of mirrors, revealing my own soul. You will grow old and gray and decrepit, while I... I will stay young, and beautiful, and safe. That is all that matters.

(DORIAN GRAY smiles, and pulls the screen in front of the portrait.)

(BLACKOUT)

ACT II
Scene 2

SETTING: The same room, the following morning.

AT RISE: DORIAN is having breakfast. ALICE ushers BASIL into the room, then exits.

ALICE
Mr. Basil Hallward to see you, Miss.

BASIL
I am so glad I have found you, Dorian. I called last night but they told me you were at the opera. Of course, I knew that was impossible but I wish you had left word where you had really gone. I passed a dreadful evening, half afraid that one tragedy might beget another. Did you go down to see the young man's mother? They gave the address in the paper and I thought of following you down there, only I was afraid of intruding upon a sorrow which I could not lighten. What a state she must be in, poor woman. Her only child, too. What did she say about it all?

DORIAN
(Who has never stopped eating her breakfast.)

My dear Basil, how should I know? I was at the opera last night. Oh, don't look at me like that, and don't talk about horrid subjects. If one doesn't talk about a thing, it has never happened. It is simply expression which gives reality to a thing. I might mention that John was not her only child. She had a young daughter who goes to boarding school or some such thing. But now, tell me about yourself and what you have been painting.

BASIL
(Stunned silence.)

You went to the opera? You went to the opera while John Vane was lying dead? You talk to me of the opera being charming before the man you claimed to love has even a quiet grave to sleep in?

DORIAN
Stop it, Basil. I won't hear it. What is done is done. What is past is past.

BASIL
You call yesterday the past?

DORIAN
What has the actual lapse of time to do with it? It is only shallow people who require years to get rid of an emotion. One who is master of herself can end a sorrow as easily as she can invent a pleasure. I don't want to be at the mercy of either emotion.

BASIL
Who are you? You look exactly the same as that wonderful girl who used to come down to my studio to sit for her picture. That Dorian was a simple, natural, affectionate creature - the most unspoiled creature in the whole world. I don't know you. You talk as if you had no heart, no pity in you at all. You act like…like Harriett.

DORIAN
I owe a great deal to Harriett, Basil. More than I owe to you. You only taught me to be vain.

BASIL
Well, I am punished for that, Dorian - or shall be some day.

DORIAN

I don't know what you mean, Basil. What is it that you want?

BASIL
I want the Dorian Gray I used to paint.

DORIAN
You have come too late. If you had come yesterday at half past five you would have found me in tears. You must not think I have not suffered. I suffered immensely. Then it passed away. You are awfully unjust, Basil. You came down here to console me. That was charming of you. But you find me consoled and you are furious. You are surprised to find me talking thus? You have not realized how I have developed. I was a schoolgirl when you knew me. I am a woman now with new passions, new thoughts, new ideas. Please, let us not quarrel, Basil. I am what I am. There is nothing more to be said.

BASIL
Well, Dorian, I won't speak to you again about this horrible subject. I only trust your name won't be mentioned in connection with it. The inquest is to take place this afternoon. Have they summoned you?

DORIAN
No. No one saw me go to his dressing room that night. But Basil, you must do me a drawing of John. I should like to have something more of him than the memory of a few kisses and some broken, pathetic words.

BASIL
I will try and do something, Dorian, if it would please you. But you must come and sit for me yourself. I can't get on without you.

DORIAN
I can never sit for you again, Basil. It is impossible.

BASIL
What nonsense? Do you mean to say you don't like what I did of you? Where is it, by the bye? Why is the screen pulled in front of it? Let me look at it. It is the best thing I have ever done. Do take the screen away, Dorian. It is simply disgraceful of your servant hiding my work like that.

DORIAN
My servant has nothing to do with it, Basil. You don't imagine I let her arrange my room for me? No; I did it myself. The light was too strong on the portrait.

BASIL
Too strong? Surely not, Dorian. This is an admirable place for it. Let me see it.

(BASIL moves toward the painting.)

DORIAN
Basil, you must not look at it. I don't wish you to.

BASIL
Not look at my own work! You are not serious. Why shouldn't I?

DORIAN
If you try to look at it, Basil, upon my word of honour I will never speak to you again as long as I live. I am quite serious. I don't offer any explanation, and you are not to ask for any. But remember, if you touch this screen, everything is over between us.

BASIL
Dorian…

DORIAN
Don't speak!

BASIL
Well, of course I won't look at it if you don't want me to. But really it seems rather absurd that I shouldn't see my own work, especially as I am going to exhibit it in Paris in the autumn.

DORIAN
Exhibit it? But you told me not a month ago that you would never exhibit it. You assured me most solemnly that nothing in the world would induce you to send it to any exhibition.

BASIL
Dorian, if you wish me to not exhibit your portrait, I won't. If you wish me never look at your picture again, I am content. I have always you to look at. Your friendship is dearer to me than any fame or reputation. You have been the one person in my life who has really influenced my art. Whatever I have done that is good, I owe to you.

DORIAN
You and I are friends, Basil, and we must always remain so.

BASIL
(Preparing to leave.)

I think you would much rather be friends with my sister.

DORIAN
Oh, Harriett. Harriett spends her days saying what is incredible and her evenings doing what is improbable. Just the sort of life I would like to lead. But still, I don't think I would go to Harriett if I were in trouble. I would sooner go to you, Basil.

BASIL
You will sit for me again?

DORIAN
Impossible.

BASIL
You spoil my life as an artist by refusing, Dorian. No man comes across two ideals in a single lifetime. Few come across one.

DORIAN
I can't explain it to you, Basil. But I must never sit for you again. There is something fatal about a portrait. It has a life of its own. I will come and have tea with you. That will be just as pleasant.

BASIL
Pleasanter for you, I am afraid. And now, goodbye. I am sorry you won't let me look at the picture once again. But that can't be helped.

(BLACKOUT)

ACT II
Scene 3

SETTING: Ten years later. The home of LADY NARBOROUGH.

AT RISE: There is a social gathering in progress. Several people are enjoying quiet conversation throughout the room. DORIAN enters. LADY NARBOROUGH greets her, takes her by the arm and escorts her into the room.

LADY NARBOROUGH
Dorian dear, I am extremely glad you could come. You have always been one of my special favorites. If I had met you when I was much younger I should have been very jealous of you. Ah, here is Alan Campbell, the Duke of Berwick. Duke this is Miss Dorian Gray.

BERWICK
We've met. Miss Gray.

DORIAN
(Suppressing a wicked smirk.)

Good evening, Alan. How are your experiments going? And how is your... wife?

BERWICK
(Obviously uncomfortable.)

And now Lady Narborough, I am afraid I must be off.

LADY NARBOROUGH
So soon? But you've just arrived.

BERWICK
Indeed, I fear I must.

(BERWICK exits abruptly.)

LADY NARBOROUGH
Young men today - they are always in such a rush. Oh, I am sorry Dorian. I know this is a rather tedious affair. I got it up in a hurry for my daughter, Helen. She came up quite suddenly from the country to stay with me. And to make matters worse, she brought her husband along. I think it is most unkind of her, my dear. You shan't sit next to either of them. You shall sit by me and amuse me.

(HARRIETT enters. LADY NARBOROUGH sees her and waves.)

And I am very put out with your friend, Lady Harriett Wotton. She is dreadfully late and she promised not to disappoint me.

(HARRIETT crosses the room to LADY NARBOROUGH and DORIAN.)

HARRIETT
Good evening Penelope. Lovely dress. Good evening Dorian. Dorian are you quite well? You seem out of sorts.

LADY NARBOROUGH
I believe she is in love.

DORIAN
Lady Narborough, I have not been in love for a whole week. I fear love is a great disappointment.

LADY NARBOROUGH
Don't tell me you have exhausted love already. When a woman says that, one knows that love has exhausted her. Lady Harriett is very wicked and I sometimes wish that I had been; but you are made to be good - you look so…good. We must find you a husband. Don't you think so, Harriett?

HARRIETT
I am always telling her so, Penelope.

LADY NARBOROUGH
We must seek out a suitable match for her. I shall go through Debrett carefully tonight and draw out a list of all the eligible bachelors. I want it to be what The Morning Post calls…a suitable alliance, and I want you both to be very happy.

HARRIETT
What nonsense people talk about happy marriage. A woman can be happy with any man, as long as she does not love him.

LADY NARBOROUGH
Harriett, you are a complete cynic.

(LADY RUXTON approaches.)

Ah, and here is Lady Ruxton! Lady Ruxton, Lady Harriett Wotton. Miss Dorian Gray.

LADY RUXTON
Charmed. You must both come and dine with me soon. I'm sure you would be much better tonic than what Sir Andrew prescribes for me. You must tell me what people you would like to meet, though. I want it to be a delightful gathering.

HARRIETT
I should be delighted to dine with you, Lady Ruxton. Invite

whomever you like. My preference is for men who have a future and women who have a past.

(There is polite laughter.)

LADY RUXTON
Which is precisely why I have invited Miss Gray. I hear the most deliciously decadent things about her past. Yet, now that I see her, I can't believe any of them are true. Why you

are still a slip of a girl. You haven't had time to do half the things attributed to you.

DORIAN
Lady Ruxton, I would find it most amusing to dine with you, but I am no slip of a girl. I achieved my majority nearly ten years ago. And as for what has been said about me…well, I admit I smoke a great deal too much.

LADY RUXTON
As do I, Miss Gray. I am going to limit myself in the future.

DORIAN
Pray don't, Lady Ruxton. Moderation is a fatal thing. Enough is as bad as a meal. More than enough is as good as a feast.

LADY RUXTON
You must come and explain that to me some afternoon, Miss Gray. It sounds a fascinating theory. You have such a charming smile and infinite grace, and yet one hears such stories.

DORIAN
Stories, Lady Ruxton?

LADY RUXTON
Tush. The prattle of jealous women pecking after a pretty

girl, that is clearly all it is. If men who have been pledged to another have thrown themselves at your feet, why, what fault is that of yours? Yet, I have heard that many who were once most intimate friends grow perfectly pallid at the mention of your name. You have a dangerous beauty I think, Dorian Gray.

DORIAN
I have a great deal of money, Lady Ruxton. That provides me with a great deal of security and a great potential for

scandal among those who do not.

LADY RUXTON
Indeed. I never listen to scandal, at least not about the very rich. Civilized society is ever ready to believe anything to the detriment of those who are both rich and fascinating, and you my dear, are both.

(BLACKOUT)

ACT II
Scene 4

SETTING: Twenty years later. The home of DORIAN GRAY. Nothing has changed. The portrait remains behind a dressing screen.

AT RISE: BASIL is sitting, waiting. DORIAN enters. She is startled, and does not recognize BASIL at first. He is thirty years older than when we first saw him. DORIAN is unchanged.

DORIAN
Who are you?

BASIL
Lord in heaven, Dorian. You haven't aged a day. I know I have, but still, surely you recognize an old friend?

DORIAN
Basil? Can it be possible? I heard you were living in Paris. What's it been - 12 years?

BASIL
More like 14. I've been waiting in your library every since nine o'clock. I finally took pity on your poor servant and told her to go to bed, that if you weren't here by midnight I would let myself out. I'm on my way back to Paris tonight. I'll be on the 2 o'clock train to the coast and then across the channel, but I particularly wanted to see you before I left.

DORIAN
I am sorry you are going away so soon, but I suppose you will be back directly?

BASIL
No. I quit London long ago. There is nothing for me here anymore. I've taken a studio in Paris and have shut myself up in it. I have these great pictures in my head that I must get onto canvas.

DORIAN
I hear your exhibits are all the rage in Paris.

BASIL
Dorian, I didn't come here to talk about myself. I have something to say to you.

DORIAN
I should be charmed to hear it, but won't you miss your train?

BASIL
I have plenty of time, and I shan't have any delays on account of my luggage for I've sent it on ahead. All I have is me, and I can easily get to Victoria in twenty minutes.

DORIAN
Very well then. But mind you, don't talk about anything serious. Nothing is serious nowadays. Can I get you anything?

BASIL
No. your servant made me quite at home before she retired. But I do wish to speak to you seriously. Don't frown like that. You make it so much more difficult for me.

DORIAN
What is it all about? I hope it not about myself. I am tired of myself tonight. I should like it to be about someone else.

BASIL
It is about yourself, and I must say it to you. I shall not keep you long. It is not too much to ask of you, Dorian, and it is entirely for your own sake that am speaking. I think you

should know that the most dreadful things are being said against you in London.

DORIAN
I don't wish to know anything about them. I love scandals about other people, but scandals about myself don't interest me. They have not got the charm of novelty.

BASIL
They must interest you, Dorian. You don't want people to talk of you as something vile and degraded. You have your position and your wealth, and all that sort of thing. But position and wealth are not everything. Mind you, I don't believe these rumors at all. I can't believe them when I see you. Sin is a thing that writes itself across a man's face. It cannot be concealed. There is no such thing as a secret sin. If a man has a vice it shows itself in the lines of his mouth, the droop of the eyelids, the molding of his hands. But you, Dorian, with your pure, bright, innocent face, and your marvelous untroubled youth - I can't believe anything against you. Yet, when I hear all these hideous things that people are whispering about you, I don't know what to say.

DORIAN
Then don't say anything, Basil.

BASIL
I Must. Why is it, Dorian, that a man like the Duke of Berwick leaves the room when you enter? Why is it that so many ladies in London will neither go to your house nor invite you to theirs? You used to be great friends with Lady Staveley. I met her at a dinner, and your name happened to come up in connection with the miniatures you lent the museum. Lady Staveley curled her lip and said that you might have the most artistic tastes, but that you were a woman that no pure-minded girl should be allowed to know, and whom no chaste man should sit in the same room with.

I reminded her that I was a friend of yours and asked her what she meant. She told me. Right out before everybody. It was horrible.

Why is your friendship so fatal to young men, Dorian? There was that wretched boy in the Guards who committed suicide. Sir Henry Ashton had to leave London with a tarnished name. What about Adrian Singleton and his dreadful end. What about Lord Kent's only son and his career? I met Kent yesterday in St. James' Street and he seemed broken with shame and sorrow. What about the young Duke of Perth? What sort of life has he got now? What lady would associate with him now?

DORIAN
Stop it, Basil. You talk of things you know nothing about. You ask me why Berwick leaves a room when I enter? It is because I know everything about his life - not because he knows anything about mine. You ask be about Henry Ashton and young Perth. Did I teach the one his vices, and the other his debauchery? If Kent's silly son takes his wife from the streets, what is that to me? If Adrian Singleton writes his friend's name across a bill, am I his keeper? And Alexis Staveley? You seem to have forgotten that we are in the native land of the hypocrite. It is enough for a woman to have distinction and brains for every common tongue to wag against her. And what sort of lives do these people like Alexis Staveley, who pose at being moral, lead themselves?

BASIL
That is not the question. England is bad enough, and English society is all wrong. That is the reason I want you to be fine. You have not been fine. One has the right to judge a person by the effect she has on her friends. Yours seem to lose all sense of honor, of goodness, of purity. You have filled them with a madness for pleasure. They have gone down into the depths, and you led them there. Yes - you led them there,

and yet you can smile as you are smiling now. And what is worse, I know you and Harriett are inseparable. Surely for that reason, if for none other, you should not have made my sister's name a byword.

DORIAN
Take care, Basil. You go too far.

BASIL
No! I will speak and you will listen. When you met Harriett she was high minded and spouted all sorts of nonsense. But not a breath of scandal ever touched her. Is there now a single decent woman in London who would drive with her in the park? Why, even her children won't come and see her. Then there are the other stories - stories that... Are they true? Can they be true? When I first heard them I laughed. I hear them now and shudder.

Don't shrug your shoulders like that. Don't be so indifferent. You have a wonderful influence. Let it be for good, not evil. They say that you corrupt every one with whom you become intimate, and that it is quite sufficient for you to enter a house for shame of some kind to follow after.

I don't know whether it is so or not. How could I know? I thought I knew you…once. I thought you were incapable of any ill action. Know you? I wonder do I know you at all? Before I could answer that I should have to see your soul.

DORIAN
See my soul?

BASIL
Yes, to see your soul. But only God can do that.

DORIAN
Do you think so? You shall see it yourself, tonight. Come - it is your own handiwork. Why shouldn't you look upon it.

You can tell the world all about it afterwards, if you dare. Nobody would believe you, and if they did, they would like me all the better for it. I know this age better than you do. Come, I tell you. You have chattered enough about corruption. Now you shall look on it face to face.

BASIL
Stop it, Dorian. You are speaking blasphemy.

DORIAN
I keep a diary of my life and it never leaves this room. I shall show it to you. Yes, I shall show you my soul, that thing you fancy only God can see. Pull back that screen and you shall see mine.

BASIL
You are mad, Dorian, or playing a part.

DORIAN
You won't do it? Then I must do it myself.

(DORIAN flings the screen to the floor revealing the painting. BASIL screams at the hideous face that leers back at him from the portrait.)

DORIAN
What is the matter, Basil? Don't you recognize your handiwork? I believe you once said it was the best thing you had ever done.

BASIL
What does this mean?

DORIAN
Years ago when I was a young, innocent girl, you met me, flattered me and taught me to be vain, and you finished a portrait of me that revealed to me the wonder of youth and beauty. In a mad moment that even now I don't know whether I regret or not, I made a wish, perhaps you would call it a prayer...

BASIL

I remember. How well I remember. No! The thing is impossible. The room is damp. Mildew has got into the canvas. The paints I used had some wretched mineral poison in them. I tell you it is impossible!

DORIAN

Ah, all things are possible to him who believes.

BASIL

You told me you had destroyed it.

DORIAN

I was wrong. It has destroyed me.

BASIL

I don't believe it is my picture.

DORIAN

Can't you see your ideal in it?

BASIL

My ideal, as you call it…

DORIAN

As you called it!

BASIL

There was nothing evil in it. Nothing shameful. You were to me such an ideal as I shall never meet again. This is the face of a Gorgon.

DORIAN

It is the face of my soul.

BASIL

Is that the face I worshipped? It has the eyes of the devil.

DORIAN

Each of us has Heaven and Hell within him, Basil.

BASIL
If this is all true, and this is what you have done with your soul…you must be worse even than those who talk against you.

(BASIL begins to shudder and weep.)

Dorian, we must pray. Pray, Dorian, pray! What is it that we were taught to say when we were young? 'Lead us not into temptation. Forgive us our sins. Wash away our iniquities.' Let us say it together. The prayer of your pride has been answered. The prayer of your repentance will be answered as well. I worshipped you too much. I am punished for it. You worshipped yourself too much. We are both punished.

DORIAN
It is too late, Basil.

BASIL
It is never too late, Dorian. Let us kneel down and see if we cannot remember a prayer. Isn't there a verse somewhere, 'Though your sins be as scarlet, yet I will make them white as snow?'

DORIAN
Those words mean nothing to me now.

BASIL
Hush! Don't say that. You have done enough evil in your life. My God, don't you see that accursed thing leering at us.

(BASIL turns and stares at the portrait, and begins to pray. DORIAN turns away and sees a letter opener on the table. She picks it up, examines it, turns back to BASIL, and walks toward him.)

DORIAN
Did God hear your prayer, Basil?

BASIL
(Without turning around.)

Yes, I believe He did?

DORIAN
So your sins are washed away? You are clean? If you died tonight your soul would go straight to heaven?

BASIL
Yes, I believe so.

DORIAN
Good.

(DORIAN stabs BASIL in the back. BASIL falls to the floor.)

(BLACKOUT)

ACT II
Scene 5

SETTING: The same room, a few minutes later. The screen has been set back up. No one is in the room.

AT RISE: There is an insistent pounding on the door. ALICE, in her night clothes, enters and goes to the door. ALICE is thirty years older than when we first met her.

ALICE
I'm coming, I'm coming. Don't get a twist in your knickers. Who is it?

DORIAN
(From outside.)

Open the door, Alice. I have forgotten my latch key.

(ALICE opens the door. DORIAN enters.)

I'm sorry to have to wake you, Alice. You look as if you've been sleeping soundly. Nothing disturbed your sleep 'til now?

ALICE
No mum. I've slept like a baby, thank you for asking.

DORIAN
My, it must be terribly late. What o'clock is it?

ALICE
(Looking at the clock)

Ten minutes past three, mum.

DORIAN
Ten minutes past three! Well, tempest fuget. You must wake

me at nine tomorrow. I have some things I need to do.

ALICE
Very good, mum.

DORIAN
Did anyone call this evening?

ALICE
Mr. Basil Hallward, mum. He left his card. He stayed here until midnight and then went to catch his train.

DORIAN
Oh! I am so sorry I didn't see him. Did he leave any message?

ALICE
No mum, except that he would write to you from Paris.

DORIAN
That will do, Alice. Don't forget to wake me at nine tomorrow.

ALICE
Yes mum.

(ALICE exits. DORIAN waits a moment to ensure ALICE is gone for the night, then moves the screen revealing the murdered BASIL slumped in a chair beside the painting.)

DORIAN
Poor Basil. It is well you died at night. Such things are for the darkness, not for the light of day. For all the world knows you are on your way to Paris, and as Alice can testify we never met here today. You left hours before I arrived at home. Still, we must do something with you. I can't have you lying around my sitting room, can I? But I can't very well get you out of here by myself, either. Who to call?

(DORIAN takes the Blue Book down from a shelf and begins turning pages, finally settling on one entry. A wicked smile crosses her face.)

Alan Campbell, the Duke of Berwick. Yes, just the man I want for this work.

(DORIAN turns back to the corpse, and sees a red stain has appeared on the hands of the portrait and is running down the canvas and dripping onto the floor.)

(BLACKOUT)

ACT II
Scene 6

SETTING: The same room, the following morning. The screen has been replaced.

AT RISE: DORIAN is sipping coffee and writing a letter. She places the letter in an envelope and seals it. ALICE enters.)

ALICE
The Duke of Berwick, mum, as you requested.

DORIAN
Ask him to come in, Alice.

ALICE
Yes, mum.

(ALICE exits and BERWICK, now twenty years older than when we last saw him, enters.)

DORIAN
Alan! How kind of you to come.

BERWICK
I had intended never to enter you house again, Miss Gray. But your letter said it was a matter of life and death.

DORIAN
Yes; it is a matter of life and death, Alan, and to more than one person. Please. Sit down.

(BERWICK sits, and there is a strained silence for a moment.)

DORIAN
I'll come right to the point, Alan. There is a dead man in this house - in point of fact, in this very room. He has been dead for ten hours now. No, don't stir, and don't look at me like that. Who the man is, why he died, and how he died are matters that do not concern you. What you have to do is this…

BERWICK
What I have to do? Oh, stop it Miss Gray. I won't hear you further. Whether what you have told me is true or not doesn't concern me. I entirely decline to be mixed up any further in your life. Keep your secrets to yourself. They don't interest me any more.

DORIAN
Alan, they will have to interest you. I am awfully sorry, but I can't help myself. You are the one man who is able to save me, so I am forced to bring you into the matter. I have no option, you see? You are scientific, Alan. You know about chemistry and things of that sort. You have made certain experiments. You have told me so. I only want you to do the same for me.

BERWICK
What kind of experiment?

DORIAN
I want you to destroy the body - destroy it so that not a vestige of it will be left. Nobody saw this person come into the house. Indeed, at this precise moment he is supposed to be in Paris. He will not be missed for months. When he is missed there must be no trace of him here. You, Alan, must change him into a handful of ashes that I may scatter into the wind.

BERWICK
You are mad, Dorian.

DORIAN
I was waiting for you to call me 'Dorian.'

BERWICK
You are mad, I tell you. Mad to imagine that I would raise a finger to help you, mad to have made this monstrous confession. Do you think I would peril my reputation for you?

DORIAN
It was suicide, Alan.

BERWICK
I am glad of that. But who drove him to it? You, I should fancy.

DORIAN
You refuse to help me?

BERWICK
Of course I refuse. I will have nothing to do with it. I don't care what shame comes to you. You deserve it. You deserve it all and more. I should not be sorry to see you publicly disgraced. You have come to the wrong man. Go to some other of your friends, if you have any left.

DORIAN
If you found this man lying on a table with gutters scooped out for the blood to flow through, you would simply look upon him as an admirable subject. You would probably feel that you were benefiting the human race by increasing the sum of knowledge. To destroy a body must be far less horrible than the hideous dissections you are accustomed to performing. All I am asking is for you to do what you have done many times before. You have never inquired where the dead things on which you experiment came from. Don't inquire now. I need you to help me, Alan. We were more than friends once, remember?

BERWICK
Don't speak of those days, Dorian. They are dead. And I have no desire to help you. I am simply indifferent to the whole thing. It has nothing to do with me.

(DORIAN crosses to her desk and picks up the envelope that contains the letter she had just written. She hands it to BERWICK. He takes it and reads it. A sense of trapped helplessness comes over him.)

DORIAN
I am so sorry for you, Alan. But you leave me no alternative. You see the address? If you don't help me, I must send it. If you don't help me, I will send it. You know what the result will be. But you are going to help me. It is impossible for you to refuse. I tried to spare you. You will do me the justice to admit that. You were stern, harsh, offensive. You treated me a no man has ever dared - no living man, at any rate. I bore it all. Now it is for me to dictate terms.

BERWICK
There are things I need from my laboratory.

DORIAN
Write them down on a sheet of paper. My servant will take a cab and fetch what you require.

BERWICK
You are infamous. Absolutely infamous.

DORIAN
Hush, Alan. You have saved my life.

BERWICK
Your life? Good heavens, what a life to save. You have gone from corruption to corruption. In doing what I am about to do it is not of your life that I am thinking.

DORIAN
I don't think I shall be able to help you with this task, Alan.

BERWICK
It is nothing to me. I don't require you. I don't want you. When I am done I will let myself out. And then let us never see each other again.

(BLACKOUT)

ACT III
Scene 1

SETTING: Ten more years have passed. A dingy box of a dingy theatre - the same theatre where DORIAN once saw a rising young actor named JOHN VANE perform.

AT RISE: HARRIETT and DORIAN enter and sit down. There is much the same chatter from the lower class audience on the orchestra level below. HARRIETT is 40 years older than when we first met her and has been ravaged by age and her addictions to alcohol and opium. DORIAN appears unchanged.

DORIAN
I still don't know why you have insisted we come here tonight, Harriett. I had thought never to set foot in this place again.

HARRIETT
To cure the soul by means of the senses, and the senses by means of the soul. That is the secret which you are always telling me these days. Theatre is the opiate of the masses, and much less expensive than the real thing. Besides the memory of old sins can be destroyed by the madness of sins that are new.

DORIAN
Harriett, I don't understand a word you are saying.

HARRIETT
To cure the soul by means of the senses. My soul is certainly sick to death. I wonder, is it true that the senses can cure it?

DORIAN
I don't know what you mean.

HARRIETT
Shhh! The curtain is rising. It is the Scottish play. The woman who plays the role of Lady MacBeth is extraordinary.

(The lights dim as the play begins. The lights rise as we hear the play is heard in voice over.)

SIBYL as LADY MACBETH (V.O.)

Infirm of purpose! Give me the daggers: the sleeping and the dead Are but as pictures: 'tis the eye of childhood That fears a painted devil. If he do bleed, I'll gild the faces of the grooms withal; For it must seem their guilt.

HARRIETT
What can atone for innocent blood, Dorian? Hmm? Ah, there is no atonement; but though forgiveness is impossible, forgetfulness is possible still, is it not?

DORIAN
Do stop talking nonsense for a moment, Harriett.

(The play continues in voice over.)

SIBYL as LADY MACBETH (V.O.)
Yet here's a spot. Out, damned spot! out, I say! One: two: why, then, 'tis time to do't.--Hell is murky!--Fie, my lord, fie! a soldier, and afeard? What need we fear who knows it, when none can call our power to account? Yet who would have thought the old man to have had so much blood in him. Will these hands ne'er be clean?

HARRIETT
Who would have thought the old man would have so much blood in him?

DORIAN
I do believe you have had too much to drink, Harriett.

HARRIETT
There is no such thing as too much, Dorian, remember? But it is not the drink that causes my throat to burn and my hands to twitch. Theatre may be the opiate of the masses, but it is the opium itself that gnaws at me. I have you to thank for this incessant hunger.

DORIAN
You begin to bore me, Harriett. I think I will go.

HARRIETT
No. I think you should stay. There is someone who wishes to meet you. And whom I wish for you to meet.

(BLACKOUT)

ACT III

Scene 2

SETTING: Dressing room of the late JOHN VANE, now occupied by SIBYL VANE. It looks much the same.

AT RISE: SIBYL is seated with her back to the door, removing her stage makeup. DORIAN and HARRIETT enter.

HARRIETT
My dear, Sibyl, you performed divinely tonight. One would think you entirely mad. Your brother would be so proud. I don't believe you have ever met my friend, though you have sought her for many years.

DORIAN
Sought me? Harriett, who is this woman? Why have you brought me here?

HARRIETT
Miss Dorian Gray, meet Sibyl Vane.

DORIAN
Sibyl Vane? John's little sister?

SIBYL
(Without turning around.)

Yes, John's little sister. John Vane, your lover, was my older brother. I adored him; worshipped the ground he walked on. I always wanted to follow him into the theatre, but he wouldn't hear of it. Said he wanted me to be a proper lady. He and mother sacrificed horribly to send me to boarding school. When he died the money ran out. Mother starved to death, and I...well, I am an actress now.

My brother killed himself. He drank poison for the love of you. His death is at your door. Make your peace, Miss Gray, for as surely as there is a God in heaven, tonight you shall join him in the grave.

(When SIBYL turns to face the other women, she has a pistol in her hand. When she sees DORIAN she stops, confused. She puts the gun down, and drops her head into her hands. She is shaken by what she almost did.)

SIBYL
My apologies, my lady. You are obviously not the one I seek. John died nearly forty years ago, and it is clear that you haven't even reached your majority. A confusion of names surely.

(DORIAN walks calmly to SIBYL and pats her on the shoulder while she picks up her gun. She backs up training the gun on SIBYL.)

HARRIETT
Fool! Why didn't you kill her when you had the chance?

SIBYL
(Look up, startled to see DORIAN with the gun.)

This is not the Dorian Gray I am looking for. She is far too young. Thank God I have not got innocent blood on my hands.

HARRIETT
Innocent? Innocent?

(Laughing bitterly, almost hysterically.)

When I first laid eyes on this woman she was a mere 17 years old. That was more than forty years ago!

DORIAN
And now Harriett, before I kill you, would you please tell me why this betrayal of our friendship?

HARRIETT
Did you think Berwick would keep silent forever? One night after consuming a prodigious amount of absinth, he pulled me aside as if I were a priest and he a penitent, trying to cleanse his soul through confession. He told me how he reduced my brother's body to pile of smoldering ash that you casually dumped into the street. You remember the night, Dorian. You commented what a pity it was that such a pillar of society had thrown himself in front of a train. And then you laughed! You may kill me now, Dorian. I don't care. I've already notified the authorities. I wonder, when they hang you, how long it will take you to die.

(Fade to black as two shots ring out.)

ACT III
Scene 3

SETTING: Later that night. DORIAN'S home.

AT RISE: DORIAN rushes in and paces nervously, looks out the window for any sign of pursuit. She pulls the screen from the portrait to reveal a skeletal figure, hideous to behold. She hears BASIL pleading for her repentance.

BASIL (V.O.)
Dorian, we must pray. Pray, Dorian, pray! What is it that we were taught to say when we were young? 'Lead us not into temptation. Forgive us our sins. Wash away our iniquities.' Let us say it together.

DORIAN
Forgive us our sins? Is that a proper prayer of a sinner in the hands of a most just God? No! An honest sinner should cry 'Smite us for our iniquities.' Besides, it is too late. I've gone too far down the road to perdition.

BASIL (V.O.)
It is never too late, Dorian. Let us kneel down and try if we cannot remember a prayer. Isn't there a verse somewhere, 'Though your sins be as scarlet, yet I will make them white as snow?'

DORIAN
Yes, I do want a new life! I will renounce evil. I loath my youth. Take it back! Do you hear me? Take it back!

(She examines the painting for any change.)

No change. None at all, save in the mouth - the curved wrinkle of the hypocrite. Is that all I am? A hypocrite?

(She laughs.)

I never could fool you, could I old friend. You know the intent and condition of my heart better than I.

BASIL (V.O.)
If we confess our sins He is faithful and just to forgive...

DORIAN
Is that all? Nothing that I do can cleanse my soul till I have confessed my sin?

(She starts to laugh.)

What sin? There is no such thing as sin. Do you hear me!?

(Changes to anger.)

None of this is my fault. Basil Hallward said unspeakable things to me. He made me suffer dreadfully. His death was a moment of madness - that is all. It seems very little to me now. John Vane and Alan Campbell died by their own hands, not mine. Sibyl Vane and Harriett Wotten conspired against me. It is not my fault, do you hear?! I'll have none of it. What need have I of forgiveness, I, who have eternal youth; eternal beauty? I am eternal! I will ascend into heaven, I will exalt myself above the stars. I am God!

The magic mirror of my soul? No more. I will be free of you.

(DORIAN picks up the knife she used to kill BASIL and faces the portrait.)

When you are dead, I will be at peace.

(She plunges the knife into the portrait's heart. Demonic laughter echoes all around her. She turns back to the audience. A look of horror comes over her face and she begins to scream as if she sees the devil himself coming for her soul, as indeed he is. Blackout as she continues to scream, then silence. The lights rise slowly to reveal the Picture of DORIAN GRAY, back to normal but with the knife still embedded in its breast, and a smoking pile of bones and ashes at the foot of the easel.)

DORIAN (V.O.)
To be forever young? Who would surrender that chance, what ever the consequences might be? I would give everything for that. I would give my very soul.

(CURTAIN)

Also Available from
WordCrafts Theatrical Press

Mark Twain Presents The Adventures of Tom Sawyer
  By Mike Parker

Jane Austen's Pride & Prejudice
  by Paula K. Parker

Jane Austen's Sense & Sensibility
  by Paula K. Parker

Charles Dickens' A Christmas Carol
  By Ronnie Meek

www.ingramcontent.com/pod-product-compliance
Lightning Source LLC
Chambersburg PA
CBHW072057290426
44110CB00014B/1723